Better Together

HARRISON HOUSE BOOKS
BY DUANE SHERIFF

Identity Theft
Our Union with Christ

Better Together

HOW TO BUILD A MARRIAGE THAT LASTS

DUANE SHERIFF

Published by Harrison House Publishers
Shippensburg, PA 17257

Cover design by Jeremy B. Ferguson, jb-ferguson.com
Interior design by Terry Clifton

ISBN 13 TP: 978-1-6803-1770-1
ISBN 13 eBook: 978-1-6803-1771-8
ISBN 13 HC: 978-1-6803-1773-2
ISBN 13 LP: 978-1-6803-1772-5

For Worldwide Distribution, Printed in the U.S.A.
2 3 4 5 6 7 8 / 25 24 23 22 21

Dedication

I dedicate this book to my wife Sue, who has been a strength in my life since 1980. We truly have been "better together" in this life journey of marriage and the covenant we entered into so many years ago.

I also dedicate this to anyone who is hungry to learn more about God's plan concerning the covenant of marriage.

Contents

Foreword

by
Jacob Sheriff, Shekinah Prince, and Angelica Roesler
A son and two daughters of the author

"Happily ever after" seems like an ending only in fairy tales, not in the real world. What begins as a passionate romance and fiery love often turns into cold-hearted cohabitation or fiery arguments that end in boredom, hurt, unforgiveness, or despair. The sunny days of newlywed bliss get overshadowed, even destroyed, by the inevitable storms of life. Is this the fate of every marriage?

Not only is the answer "No!" to that question, but there is also far more than "just making it" in marriage. There is hope for a healthy marriage, but it won't be easy, nor will it follow a fairy tale script or story line. "The road to a healthy marriage is under constant construction" is a crucial statement from the pages you are about to read. A strong, healthy marriage is possible, but not without knowledge and work, plus a lot of grace. All of which you will find in this book.

In Dad's honest and straightforward style, he lays out what it takes for your marriage to be strong and healthy, even in the midst of great trials and storms. What he teaches is not theory from his head, but real-life principles from his life and marriage learned from his blood, sweat, tears, and the Word of God. One of the greatest gifts my parents gave my siblings and me was a healthy marriage. Their healthy marriage created a healthy home for my siblings and me. It gave us a vision of what a healthy marriage looks like (when marriages were crumbling all around us). Their marriage laid the foundation that made it possible for me to build upon to have a healthy marriage and to raise my children with the same vision of marriage—marked by love, commitment, humility, and hard work. My dad's genuine and forthright instruction on building a healthy marriage has become a generational blessing for myself and my siblings to pass on to our children.

I witnessed firsthand my parents navigating the challenges of careers, ministry, kids, responsibilities, trials, and storms and yet maintaining their marriage as healthy. My dad has always been willing to tell the honest truth (even to our embarrassment as kids) about everything he teaches. He makes no claim to be perfect or have the perfect marriage. He is quick to throw himself (and sometimes my mom) under the bus of honesty and transparency to show that being perfect is not required for a healthy marriage. There are fundamental anchors he teaches here that make a marriage healthy, and perfection is not one of them. Anyone who wants to do the work can have a healthy marriage—but it will not be automatic or by default, and it will not happen through romance scriptwriters. If you are willing to do the hard work, trust God, and stick with it, you can have a healthy marriage too.

If you are single and hope to be married, then you can learn principles you can put into practice today that will lead to a healthy marriage one day. If you are married but struggling, then what you are about to read can give you the needed hope and tools to build (or rebuild) a healthy marriage. If you are happily married (newlywed or otherwise), then maintaining the joy of marriage doesn't happen by accident. You will be encouraged and strengthened by my dad's words. My parents' marriage and their teaching have impacted generations in our family, and I believe it can impact generations in yours as well. You and your spouse truly are better together. And this book will show you how.

JACOB SHERIFF

Marriage is a beautiful gift, ordained and orchestrated by God to represent Christ and His church. There are no two people who have modeled to me what it means to be *Better Together* more than my parents. One of my father's greatest passions is teaching couples how to have healthy relationships growing in Christ. I know that everyone who reads this book will be blessed and equipped to have a prosperous marriage.

SHEKINAH PRINCE

When I look at my past, it is hard to believe that my parents let me marry an eighteen-year-old while I was also eighteen. My fiancé and I were young, so we knew we should go through premarital counseling (It was obvious!). Dad took it upon himself to lead our sessions. I am sure we had several different sessions with him, but the one thing I really remember from those meetings was one piece of advice. This guidance has stuck with me for over ten years. He said,

"Guys, look, it's really simple. You have to learn to change and grow *together*. Because both of you *will* change. If you don't do that together, then that's when you will start heading toward trouble."

At the time when I heard this from my dad, I thought I knew everything (as most eighteen-year-olds do) and I remember thinking, "What? We won't change! What would ever change?" Well, thank goodness Dad had given us this guidance and that I remembered it! It did not take long after our marriage began for things to start changing (like our jobs and where we lived). That simple sentence really helped me work through difficult times. It was a reminder that if I stayed in communication with this person with whom I am in a covenant relationship (my husband), then I would continually be getting to know and grow alongside him as we both changed throughout our marriage to become *Better Together*.

So my hope for you as the reader is that at least one thing in this book will stick with you and be something that could change your marriage and life forever.

ANGELICA ROESLER

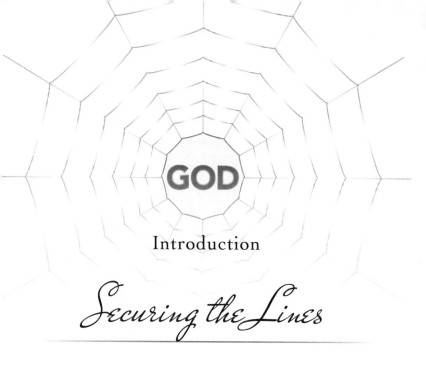

Introduction

Securing the Lines

"THE WEB OF MARRIAGE"

One day in my barn, I noticed two spider webs—a larger one and a smaller one. They were stunning works of art, examples of God's handiwork, and so I carefully let them be.

The next day, we had a bad storm. Trees blew over, and debris scattered about the property. I went back out to the barn to check on a few things and noticed the big spider web. A few of the lines were broken and flapping in the wind, but it had survived the storm. The spider was already diligently repairing it.

The smaller spider web was gone. Its anchor lines—the ones holding it to the world around it—had not been secured, and so it had blown away completely.

Just like a spider's web needs secure anchor lines to perform at its best, every marriage needs its own anchor lines that will allow the relationship to be healthy, secure, and easily repaired. The One holding these lines together—the Almighty God—sits at the center. The lines run through Him and come from Him, and it is only through His steadfast presence that a marriage can reach its utmost potential.

A strong, anchored marriage is an unstoppable force. A healthy marriage means a healthy home. Healthy homes mean healthy churches. And healthy churches mean cities that are impacted by God. These are the spiritual threads that require the firm foundation of a Christ-centered marriage.

Matthew 7:24–29 instructs us to build our lives on the rock that is the Lord Jesus Christ. If we build our lives on His Word, we will overcome the winds of adversity that will surely come. This command includes our marriages, but so few of us have the correct anchor lines needed to help our marriages succeed. A disagreement comes, and we're scrambling to fix the web with no anchor lines to grab hold of! Money troubles, hectic schedules, differing visions for the future—these threaten our marriages and leave us wondering if we can survive the storms of life.

"Can our web even be repaired? Will we make it?" You may have found yourself crying out to God with these pains. I'm here to tell you that yes, your web can be repaired. Yes, you can withstand all the storms yet to come, but only if you have the proper anchor lines in place.

You may be carrying with you some pains from a past divorce and a marriage that simply could not weather the storm. God longs to heal you and help you become properly equipped for a new marriage relationship or any other plan He has for your life.

You may be single, longing for a marriage relationship and wisely choosing to use this time to prepare your mind and heart. I'm here to remind you that in his singleness, Paul spoke truth into others' marriages. In 1 Corinthians 7, he wrote honestly about marriage and has helped millions of people since with his wisdom. You, too, can be a resource of revelation for others, helping those who are in the midst of a marriage without anchor lines.

Or you may be married, longing for a firm foundation, longing for a way to repair a broken web. I'm here to tell you that these anchor lines will give you so much more than that. It's not just about survival and getting through the years together. There is beauty and power in marriage.

God can use your union in mighty ways if you open yourself up to His anchor lines. God's plan is for you to be not only married, but also *happily* married and thriving together in life as one.

THE GOODNESS OF MARRIAGE

In reading Genesis 1, it's fascinating to discover how God created different things each day and considered them good. He created galaxies and planets and heaven itself and called them good. He created water and trees and animals and man and called them all good. On day six, after God created everything that we see on planet earth, with man as the apex of His creation, He pronounced it all *very* good.

But then something was *not* good—the man was a bachelor. The Lord said in Genesis 2:18, *"It is not good for the man to be alone. I will make a helper who is just right for him"* (NLT).

God understood that a man and a woman are better together than alone. Ecclesiastes says that two people are better than one because each can help the other succeed. If one person falls, the other can encourage. The verses go on to teach us that it is even more important to have God at the center of a relationship, because a three-fold cord (with God as the middle cord) is not quickly broken (Ecclesiastes 4:9–12).

By living together according to God's Word and loving each other as God has called and created them to do, a husband and wife can withstand life's many battles. Together, with God at the center, they can stand back to back, defending one another and conquering the enemy. There is no greater unity and no greater power of unity than a husband and a wife dwelling together in the Word of God, holding fast to their anchor lines, keeping their web secure.

Deuteronomy 32:30 speaks to the incredible strength that two people bring to a fight: *"How could one person chase a thousand of them, and two people put ten thousand to flight, unless their Rock had sold them, unless the Lord had given them up?"* (NLT).

But with this strengthened relationship will come attacks from the enemy. This is not by accident; it's by design. The devil understands the power of a godly, anchored marriage. He hates this union more than any institution or person on this planet. And because he hates the institution God put into place, he seeks to assault our marriages, using anything he can to damage our webs and cause division between us as husband and wife.

THREATS AND DANGERS TO OUR MARRIAGES

There are three primary factors that the devil uses to disrupt and destroy our marriages. The first is *lack of knowledge.*

Hosea 4:6 says, *"My people are destroyed for lack of knowledge"* (KJV). This is God's commentary for how good people who love God and love each other are failing in their marriage because their web is collapsing. Without proper knowledge of God, our marriages cannot hold up. They crumble at the slightest wind.

We, too often, lack basic biblical understanding of what husbands, dads, wives, and moms are supposed to be. We start families without knowing the purpose of marriage or that of the family unit. There is a generation of young people who simply have not been taught how to have a healthy, lasting marriage. They don't even know to include God in their relationships. The devastating results are more failed marriages, more brokenness, and more distance between us and God's plan. Believe it or not, what we don't know can hurt us.

The second contributing factor to failed marriages is *false information*. From a young age, many of us have been fed false information about marriage. We don't even realize it's happening, but every day the world influences our thinking. Man's philosophies and traditions spoil us, and our view of God's sacred institution is distorted. We bring these untruths into our relationships, and we wrongly try to model our marriages after them. The result is a worldly-anchored union that cannot withstand the devil's attacks rather than a God-anchored union that can.

First Peter 3:7 (AMPC) is clear on how a husband should live with his wife:

> *In the same way you married men should live considerately with [your wives], with an intelligent recognition [of the marriage relation], honoring the woman as [physically] the weaker, but [realizing that you] are joint heirs of the grace (God's unmerited favor) of life, in order that your prayers may not be hindered and cut off, [otherwise you cannot pray effectively].*

Both are joint heirs of God's grace. Both must show respect and honor. The world does not always think this way; the world perverts the truth, convincing us that we can ignore the marriage relationship. We can ignore how we treat one another. We can ignore what the Word of God says about the home and how it functions. This false information convinces us that these things do not matter to God. Obviously, an intelligent recognition of the marriage relation is important if it affects our prayers.

The third contributing factor to failed marriages is *neglect*. Marriages that thrive take intentional effort. Every one of us has competing priorities, including marriage, children, friends, work, and hobbies. By focusing on one, we end up ignoring the rest. We choose work over spouse, hobbies over children, and children over spouse.

Before we know it, our web is fatally damaged and the enemy has taken a foothold. We have allowed everything but our spouse and our joint relationship with God to be our focus, and the devil has encroached. Paying attention to our spouse and our basic needs as husband and wife is essential to our success in being happily married. Healthy marriages do not happen by accident, but rather by design. The road to a healthy marriage is under constant construction.

THE ANCHOR LINES

The wonderful news is that your lack of knowledge can be brought to a fullness of understanding, your false information can be corrected and lined up with His Word, and your neglect can turn into intentional living. It all starts with implementing six anchor lines that will strengthen your marriage and allow God to be at the center.

These six anchor lines of what I'm calling the "web of marriage" are areas married people must be working on throughout their lives together. This book provides an overview of each of the six areas, including insights into how to secure the anchor lines of your marriage. Then, at the end of each chapter, workbook sections will give you tools to begin applying these lessons. These tools would also work well for a small group setting.

Each anchor line, when neglected, is a cause of marital breakdown, which is far too common. While each anchor line I discuss here could fill an entire book, my purpose is to introduce these areas and encourage you to continue to grow in each as you pursue being happily married. Those lines are:

1. Security and Trust
2. Communication
3. Forgiveness and Repentance
4. Finances
5. Roles and Responsibilities
6. Sex and Romance

Just as a spider makes sure certain lines of its web are strong and secure, these six lines must be strong and secure in our marriages. Without any one of them, the marriage is vulnerable to attack. By contrast, with these anchor lines, the marriage will be healthy, strong, and able to withstand the greatest of storms.

As a parent or grandparent, these six anchor lines help get our children and grandchildren to the marriage altar. These foundational kingdom principles will equip and prepare our families to be happily and successfully married. There is a seventh anchor line that involves child training. That is a subject I will deal with in another book about "children as arrows."

WORKBOOK

Introduction Questions

Question: What makes marriage inherently good as God designed it? Describe a time when you have witnessed or experienced what it means to be better together in your marriage.

Question: How and why does satan target marriages? Which danger—lack of knowledge, false information, or neglect—poses the greatest threat to your own marriage right now? How have you fought and been victorious together against one or more of these dangers?

Question: Would you say that God is at the center of your marriage? If yes, how do you know? If no, what steps can you take to make Him central in your relationship?

Action: Look at the list of six anchor lines. Interview a couple who have been happily married for several decades. How have these anchor lines helped their marriage weather the storms of life?

Chapter One

Security and Trust

Security and trust in marriage come from two crucial components—shared commitment and shared understanding. When a couple agrees that they are completely committed to each other, no matter what, and understands mutually the purpose and goals of their union, the relationship can be built on a foundation that lasts.

My wife, Sue, and I knew when we stood at the altar that we would face problems in our marriage. We weren't naïve, but we were mutually confident in our commitment to one another and to God. We have always known that problems are opportunities to engage with God and watch Him work situations out. He gets the glory, and our marriage is strengthened.

The anchor line to security and trust is learning how to engage with Jesus together whenever storms and difficulties arise in a marriage. Our shared commitment and mutual understanding were that whatever came our way, we would work it out and walk it out together, with the Lord's help.

When Jesus was asleep in the boat in Mark 4, the storm was tossing the boat everywhere. The disciples nearly drowned before Jesus woke up and stilled the wind and the waves. Just as having Jesus in the boat wasn't an assurance of safety and security, having Jesus in a marriage doesn't mean that the marriage will last. Not every Christian couple understands this. Many have the incorrect assumption that they are guaranteed a stable marriage just because they are both born-again Christians. But if that were true, the divorce rate among Christians wouldn't be as high as we see it to be today.

The path to security and trust is learning how to engage with Christ whenever storms and difficulties arise. We need Jesus in the boat, but we also need to engage with Him in the storm.

SHARED COMMITMENT BRINGS SECURITY

In Hebrews 11:13–15—the roll call of faithful saints—the writer refers to the early believers as *"strangers and pilgrims on the earth"* and then states, *"Truly if they had called to mind that country from which they had come out, they would have had opportunity to return."* It wasn't God's will that those saints return to the place they had been. Rather, He wanted them to be focused on the future and what lay ahead. Thankfully, they did exactly that and found favor with God. If they had looked back, they would have given satan the opportunity to tempt them to go back to a place of bondage and pain.

In the same way, we must always be moving forward in our marriage and never give in to the temptation to go back. Looking back—finding an escape route—should never be an option.

Sue and I have had a successful marriage, even through trials, because we refuse to look back. We refuse to use verbiage that would even create the impression of insecurity in our marriage. We are mutually committed and secure in our relationship, and from that point of strength, we can face anything together.

How does this look for your marriage? Are you confident that your spouse is committed to the long term? Are you committed to the long term, and have you communicated that commitment?

Shared commitment is the anchor line agreement that marriage is a steadfast commitment for a lifetime. It's not a trial period simply to see if there is chemistry. It's not a temporary agreement until the kids are out of the house or interests change. It's a commitment until death.

SHARED UNDERSTANDING BRINGS TRUST

Shared understanding speaks to the covenant of marriage. In Malachi 2:13–14, the Lord tells the people that they have been rebellious in their lack of tithing and their attitudes in worship. Then, He brings up marriage. The Lord tells them: *"It is because the Lord is the witness between you and the wife of your youth. You have been unfaithful to her, though she is your partner, the wife of your marriage covenant"* (NIV).

The marriage covenant is a sacred oath, taken before God and family and friends, and it must lead to a shared understanding that marriage is holy and created to last. The covenant of marriage causes two people to become one flesh (Genesis 2:24). In this holy bond, death is the only thing to separate the spouses. Jesus indicates marriage to be an unbreakable bond:

> But *"God made them male and female" from the beginning of creation. "This explains why a man leaves his father and mother and is joined to his wife,*

and the two are united into one." Since they are no
longer two but one, let no one split apart what God
has joined together (Mark 10:6–9 NLT).

Understanding this should completely reframe your marriage. It should remove any doubts that you may have about the importance of staying and fighting for your marriage. By getting married, you made an unbreakable promise to God and to each other, and He expects you to keep that promise. When two people grab hold of this anchor line, a great sense of trust is established. You *know* that your marriage is much bigger than you and your partner. God is involved, and He will help you succeed. When divorce is no option, you fight harder and more wisely for the marriage.

SECURITY FOR ALL

You may be wondering, then, how this affects marriages in which one of the participants is a Christian and the other is not. Though Paul discourages believers from marrying nonbelievers (2 Corinthians 6:14–18), it's not considered a sin. Instead, Paul acknowledges the great difficulties that can come out of an unequally yoked marriage.

In these marriages, each person brings a different understanding and possibly different views of the importance of marriage. This results in two different—and at times competing—foundations. Without a shared foundation, a marriage struggles to have true fellowship and communion.

If marriage is built on the foundation of respect and trust with shared commitment, then that means there is intimacy in shared conversation (shared understanding). But how do you have shared conversation if there are two foundations? How can you agree with someone whose worldview is not in alignment with yours? These are just some of the difficulties of the unequally yoked marriage.

Shared understanding *is* possible within this type of marriage if you put yourself in each other's shoes and if you consider each other's perspective. It requires both of you to offer compassion and empathy as you endeavor to understand each other despite your different beliefs. Understanding where you are both coming from and how your views may differ can help with communication as you work toward a shared commitment. Find the common values you do have and build from there.

You may be reading this and feeling the pain of your own unequally yoked marriage. You may be thinking that your marriage is done for, that there is no way the two of you will come to any sort of shared commitment or shared understanding. You may be thinking that this particular anchor line just won't work for you and that it's impossible to have true security and trust with your partner.

You must hear me when I say this: God cares for your marriage. He doesn't view you as having failed or missed the mark. Instead, He wants you to view your marriage the way He does—as an opportunity to show His great love for your spouse.

God loves you as much as He loves your marriage partner. He won't forsake you on this journey of special love. He can make a way. Do you *trust* Him to do that? Are you *secure* in His promises? First Corinthians 7:12–14 says:

> *If a fellow believer has a wife who is not a believer and she is willing to continue living with him, he must not leave her. And if a believing woman has a husband who is not a believer and he is willing to continue living with her, she must not leave him. For the believing wife brings* **holiness** *to her marriage, and the believing husband brings* **holiness** *to his marriage* (NLT).

God will work in your marriage as you trust Him. Your faith is greater than any unbelief of a spouse. You and God are the majority.

ANCHOR LINE 1

Security and Trust

As with all relationships, but especially the marriage relationship, the first anchor line of security and trust is crucial to building a marriage that lasts. Whether you are going into your first marriage, have been married a long time, or have struggled through the pain of divorce but seek to be married again, developing a shared commitment and understanding with your spouse or spouse-to-be is important. We need to build healthy, happy marriages so that we can in turn have healthy, happy relationships with those around us. No matter where you and your spouse are on this beautiful journey of marriage, the Lord will help you to communicate well and share a life in God's goodness.

WORKBOOK

Chapter One Questions

Question: Do you and your spouse have a shared commitment to your marriage? Do you ever talk about divorce in a flippant or threatening way? Are you both in this relationship for the long haul? How have you communicated that to each other?

Question: In the same way, we must always be moving forward in our marriage and never giving in to the temptation to go back. What are some ways that a person might be tempted to "go back," and what might be the consequences? How will you keep a forward focus in your marriage?

Question: What are some of the difficulties that you have observed in an unequally yoked marriage (either your own or that of someone you know)? If such a marriage is to be successful, what mindsets will be necessary?

Action: For further study on covenants, please visit pastor-duane.com and search "covenant" in our messages.

Together, study the biblical and historical basis of a covenant (compared to a contract). How is the covenant in Genesis 15 between God and mankind unique? What does it mean that your marriage is a covenant before God? Plan a time to renew your vows with this new understanding of a covenant relationship.

Security and Trust

GOD

Chapter Two

Communication

Telephone was a fun game to play when I was younger. We'd line up a group of people, and the first person would come up with a sentence. He/she would whisper that sentence to the next person, who would whisper it to the next, and so on. By the time the sentence had moved through the chain to the last person, it was oftentimes distorted, incorrect, and very humorous. Somewhere along the line, the truth had been lost. The communication had failed. A whole new narrative was birthed.

This is an overly simplistic analogy for the complexities of human interaction, but it's also very relatable. How often has what you said been misinterpreted or misconstrued by others—even by the people who know you best? I have failed many times in this area, and the outcome has never been good.

Communication is a confounding mystery and, oftentimes, a main reason why couples fight or become frustrated with one another. God never intended it to be this way. He wants communication to be simple. He wants us to have clarity. He wants truth to prevail, not imaginary narratives to rule the day.

In 2 Corinthians 11:3, Paul writes, *"But I fear, lest by any means, as the serpent beguiled Eve through his subtilty, so your minds should be corrupted from the simplicity that is in Christ"* (KJV). Because of satan and the weakness of our flesh, we will always struggle with communication. But we can minimize the threat this poses to our marriages if we work on establishing the anchor line of communicating as God intended. Satan wants to corrupt simple things, making mountains out of molehills in our marriage relation.

Even though we may find it hard to communicate effectively, God has provided four basic communication elements that are intrinsic to all of us. They are:

- Talking (Ephesians 4:29–32)

- Listening (James 1:19)
- Asking questions and providing feedback (Genesis 3:9, 11, 13)
- Being honest (Ephesians 4:15; Colossians 3:9)

Let's dive a little deeper into these four elements so that we can secure this second anchor line for a stronger, healthier marriage.

TALKING

Talking, in its best form, is a verbal sharing of one's thoughts or heart in a way that is easily understood by others.

Sometimes in marriage—and sometimes in life—you may be sharing your heart only to find the listener didn't understand a thing you said. This can happen quite often between men and women. In the world's eyes, communication between a man and a woman should be the same, right? Wrong. No matter what the world says, men and women aren't the same. God created and wired us differently. This doesn't make one better than the other. Just different. And if we don't understand the differences, we experience disconnect in our communication.

Men and women bond and communicate differently. Women bond through love, nurturing, and caring. Men bond through respect. If we don't know how to talk to each other according to those qualities, then everything about communication breaks down. If the man talks without love or caring, he isn't effective, and if the woman talks without respect, she isn't effective.

In Ephesians 5:33, the Lord's command to husbands and wives is to create healthy and mutual honor for their marriage: *"So again I say, each man must love his wife as he loves himself, and the wife must respect her husband"* (NLT). Notice that the verse starts out with "again I say." Paul has been emphasizing these two issues throughout the chapter and still feels the need to repeat them. Repeating things over and over contributes to effective communication.

On top of this, women talk for different reasons than men. For the most part, women talk through problems. It's how they process; it's part of how God made them. Men, on the other hand, talk to solve a problem. I know this to be true about me! If I enter a conversation, I'm bringing a solution.

Early in our marriage, this caused issues. Sue wanted to talk just to talk—*really*? I constantly interrupted her to fix what I perceived as a problem. She didn't want me to solve anything, but to listen. When I used to come home, Sue would say, "Can we talk?" I responded with, "About what? Is there a problem?" She just wanted to talk. Over time I have improved at listening without trying to solve her problems. Men are often to the point, whereas women tend to like to explore options and thoughts or feelings.

Adding to this problem are the methods by which we choose to communicate in these modern times. Instead of going to a person directly, we try to solve or discuss things through social media. We shoot off a text or write an email. We hide behind modern technology and then wonder why our messages fall on deaf ears. We are so afraid to speak directly, so afraid of confrontation or disagreements. We have lost the art of lovingly looking someone in the eye and committing to share our heart and work things out.

And when we do this, when we talk directly, we must uplift and encourage. We must be kind and calm. We must be loving and respectful, even if the discussion makes us want to be anything but.

Ephesians 4:29 offers a standard for good communication. The charge is to *"let no corrupt word proceed out of your mouth, but what is good for necessary edification, that it may impart grace to the hearers."* God wants us to communicate with our spouse in a way that edifies and displays grace. That's hard to do—especially if it involves having difficult or crucial conversations. But difficult conversations are a part of life. They need to happen, and as we understand more about the anchor line of communication, we begin to understand how to extend grace to one another when we talk.

I'm amazed at how often hurtful words can sneak in between a husband and wife. Ephesians 4:30–32 encourages us to be in communion with the Holy Spirit and to seek right communication with others and our spouse. We must put away *"all bitterness, wrath, anger, clamor, and evil speaking,"* and *"be kind to one another, tenderhearted, forgiving one another, even as God in Christ forgave you."* These gentle instructions show us, God's people, how we should relate to our spouse.

You need to be *tenderhearted*. You need to be *kind* even if you are discussing something hard that may come across harsh. You need to find the *grace* of God and the kindness in communication. It's okay to vent, but there should be no room for shouting or acting out in anger. Even if something is true regarding your spouse, it must be spoken in love for the relationship to grow (yes, I said grow) in the right direction (Ephesians 4:15).

It's pretty obvious to look out for harsh words and to extend grace as you're talking through problems. But there are two facets of communication that don't get enough attention—and they can wreak havoc on a marriage.

Verbal Counterpunching

I've noticed something I call "verbal counterpunching" show up in most marriages. This happens when each person jumps into the conversation and offers their opinion in the form of an attack, without truly seeking to work things out. It's like hitting a punching bag. They jump in, throw a punch, and jump away.

Instead of talking and listening and trying to fix an issue, one person is talking while the other is sitting there, looking at their spouse, thinking: *"Hurry up already. Run out of breath. Get to your point because I have something to say!"* And sure enough, the minute the other person stops talking, *BAM!* The spouse who was supposed to be listening jumps in with an attack. It's a verbal counterpunch. It's the difference between talking *to* or talking *at* someone.

This goes back and forth while the conversation goes nowhere. People are talking, but not communicating.

Remember, the number one key in communication is talking. We should never get to a place where we *think* we are talking while all we are doing is fighting or arguing. If we're fighting, we're actually grieving the Holy Spirit—the very person we need to be active and help us out of whatever disagreement we may be in.

Nonverbal Communication

Nonverbal communication is another thing that can wreak havoc, but not in the way that you're thinking. We have been trained to think that nonverbal cues are absolute. We may assume that someone with their arms crossed is angry or closed off or that someone who looks up and to the right is lying. We may think that someone who is silent is upset.

But these are not true for everyone all of the time. When we give off these cues in our relationships, we can communicate a wrong message about how we're really thinking and feeling. We need to be mindful of our body language when we're talking to others, and we also need to extend grace when our spouse or someone we're conversing with sends us one of these signals.

Not everyone with their arms crossed is mad, though that could be saying something less than positive. Not everyone who looks up and to the right when talking is lying. Not everyone who goes silent is upset. They may be struggling with processing what they are hearing. While we need to be sensitive to nonverbal conversations and signs, we should never be judgmental or accusatory.

My oldest daughter taught me the power of nonverbal communication. She was around six or seven years old, and I was bringing her home from school. She asked me if I was mad at her. I assured her that I wasn't but asked why she thought that. She told me that I looked mad and was quiet. Honestly, I was deep in thought and apparently had a mad look on my face. I didn't know what I looked like when deep in thought, having never looked at myself in the mirror while meditating. I tried to reassure her that I was not mad at her but just thinking. She was not convinced and kept accusing me of being mad to the point it almost became an option. She finally agreed reluctantly, and I tried to smile while still deep in thought. Obviously, this was an area of nonverbal communication that I needed to work on!

Whatever situation you walk into, you must exercise emotional intelligence and maturity when talking and sharing. Open yourself up to the Spirit for His guidance. Over time, Sue and I have learned each other's nonverbal communications. Study your spouse in love to learn how to hear what is being said through nonverbal communications. With me, if I get too quiet too long, something is bothering me. With Sue, if she has gone into silence, then she is processing something and needs the space.

LISTENING

Not only do we need to learn how to talk, but we also need to learn how to be quiet and to listen. James wrote, *"My dear brothers and sisters, take note of this: Everyone should be quick to listen, slow to speak and slow to become angry"* (James 1:19 NIV).

Listening is a lost art. It's part of the reason why verbal counterpunching is so prevalent in many relationships.

We need to learn to truly listen and hear the other person out. We need to take a risk and overcome the fear of being wrong or having to change our mind. The goal of listening is to understand each other, not declare who is right or wrong. We should desire to come to a place of unity and love, not division, hurt, or pain. We want a win–win solution, not a lose–win proposition. Remember, you're not trying to win an argument but rather to reconcile a breach in the relationship and to clear up any confusion or misunderstanding.

There are two components that go into truly listening to someone and hearing them out.

Choice

If your brain didn't have the ability to wipe out stimuli, you would lose your mind. If you heard everything at the same time—all the chatter and noise and chaos going on around you—you would go crazy. Every day, we choose what we listen to, and we ignore the rest. That is why *choosing* to listen to the good things is important.

You will not hear someone until you choose to hear them, and this is why we see good marriages collapsing. We see couples who love God and claim to love each other part ways because they quit listening and they quit choosing to hear one another. All of this can contribute to a marriage faltering that had once been strong and healthy.

Until you choose to hear what your spouse is saying, you won't hear it. More importantly, you must choose to listen to God, or you won't hear Him. Mark 4:9 says, *"He who has ears to hear, let him hear!"* The word *let* is the key to this verse and key to a life and marriage of prosperity.

Bringing awareness to the things you listen to is crucial to developing the anchor line of communication. You must choose to listen to the Holy Spirit. You must choose to listen to your spouse. And from there, you can work on understanding them.

Understanding

When Jesus said, *"Whoever has ears to hear, let them hear"* (Mark 4:9 NIV), He wasn't just talking about hearing what comes from the Holy Spirit. He was talking about *understanding* those words and striving to find the intention behind them.

The Spirit is there to guide you as you listen to your spouse. He is there to help you unpack what they're saying (and not saying). He is there to provide revelation from God and insight into the heart of man—the heart of your husband or wife.

This step of understanding is so very important to having the correct response to your spouse. The Spirit will guide you through understanding. But you must listen to your spouse and to God.

When You Can't Hear

Anger, hurt, fear, frustration—these feelings can prevent us from listening and hearing. When we're in this state of mind, we choose not to understand our spouse, our children, or our coworkers, and that's why so many of our relationships don't last. It's why our children are estranged from us, and it's why we have trouble getting along with people at work or at church. This is why *choosing* to hear and to *understand* are so very important. Even when we disagree with someone, we can hear them out. We can listen to their side, we can understand where they're coming from, and we can choose how to proceed, even if in the end we still disagree.

As Mark 4:24–25 says, *"Pay close attention to what you hear. The closer you listen, the more understanding you will be given"* (NLT). We must pay close attention to what we hear from our spouse. The closer we listen, the more we will understand. There's a warning here, though—if we choose not to hear and listen, then we will lose what little understanding we have. The second half of Mark 4:25 says, *"But for those who are not listening, even what little understanding they have will be taken away from them"* (NLT). When we quit listening to God and to each other, we go backward in our relationships. We can actually lose the little understanding we do have.

Mark 4:3–8 is a profound parable Jesus taught:

> *Listen! A farmer went out to plant some seed. As he scattered it across his field, some of the seed fell on a footpath, and the birds came and ate it. Other seed fell on shallow soil with underlying rock. The seed sprouted quickly because the soil was shallow. But the plant soon wilted under the hot sun, and since it didn't have deep roots, it died. Other seed fell among thorns that grew up and choked out the tender plants so they produced no grain. Still other seeds fell on fertile soil, and they sprouted, grew, and produced a crop that was thirty, sixty, and even a hundred times as much as had been planted!* (NLT)

Mark 4:13–20 encompasses the significance and explanation of the parable. Verse 13 declares, *"If you can't understand the meaning of this parable, how will you understand all the other parables?"* (NLT). Notice how understanding is progressive. When you have this understanding, you can now get more. He goes on to explain the parable as follows: *"The farmer plants seed by taking God's word to others. The seed that fell on the footpath represents those who hear the message, only to have Satan come at once and take it away"* (Mark 4:14 NLT).

Mark doesn't explain how satan steals the Word, but Matthew does in his commentary on the same parable: *"The seed that fell on the footpath represents those who hear the message about the Kingdom and don't understand it. Then the evil one comes and snatches away the seed that was planted in their hearts"* (Matthew 13:19 NLT).

God's Word is seed that is sown into our hearts and can change our lives, but if not understood, satan steals it. Our hearts are the ground in which the seed is sown, but the seed will not profit us if we do not understand; we remain fruitless.

How is it that the devil can steal the very thing God intended for us? Just as the apostle Paul talks about how lost people are blind to salvation, the devil seeks to destroy the relationship Christians have with Jesus and their spouses (2 Corinthians 4:4). The devil will use anything he can to make us become unfruitful in our relationships—even if it means distorting the truth. God is speaking into our lives and desires to bring us into greater understanding.

The devil wants you to misunderstand God and His Truth, and he wants you to misunderstand your spouse, too. He knows that the more you understand what God is saying to you, the more change you will see in your life. And the more change you see, the more difficult it will be for the devil to get a foothold. The more we listen to and understand our spouse, the more powerful a force of prayer we will have against satan and his strategies—and the more fruitful we will become in our marriage relationship.

ASKING QUESTIONS AND PROVIDING FEEDBACK

Effective talking and listening don't happen overnight. It's a process, and there aren't any shortcuts. I've seen couples decide to practice their communication only to come out of things more confused than ever. They misinterpreted, misunderstood, and mistook what the other was saying. This is why *feedback* is such an important part of the process. It offers loving accountability to ensure that what you're saying and what is being heard are one and the same. Many times, what is said is not always what is heard. How does the speaker know what is heard without feedback?

I discovered years ago that God communicates effectively by asking questions. For example, in Genesis 3:9, after Adam had sinned, God asked, *"Where are you?"* God knew where Adam was, but Adam did not know. The line of questioning helped Adam process where he was and how to get out of the mess he created. Adam said he was afraid and hid himself because he was naked. God asked in Genesis 3:11, *"Who told you that were naked? Have you eaten from the tree of which I commanded you that you should not eat?"* God went on to ask Eve a question as well (Genesis 3:13).

Jeremiah is another example of this effective tool of communication. Jeremiah 1:11–12 says, *"Moreover the word of the Lord came to me, saying, 'Jeremiah, what do you see?' And I said, 'I see a branch of an almond tree.' Then the Lord said to me 'You have seen well, for I am ready to perform My word.'"* If we asked more questions and received feedback, maybe we could discern whether what we said was heard (understood) and received well. There are three important questions to ask your spouse during communication, especially crucial conversations:

- What was said?
- What was heard?
- What was meant?

This process of each person verifying what the other person has said will enhance your marriage relationship by securing the anchor line of communication. However, these questions aren't only for the marriage relationship. I have discovered that healthy feedback must be created between people in any kind of relationship, whether with your boss, your children, or your family and friends. Most importantly, though, healthy feedback should be created between a husband and wife. Our communication with God is no different. What did God say? What did you hear? What did God mean? These questions must be asked to properly apply God's Word. It is also the same for the marriage relationship.

Feedback was a new concept for me in my marriage. I had never seen it modeled in any of the couples I knew growing up, so it seemed foreign and awkward. When I married Sue, I had no desire to give or ask for feedback in our communication. It just didn't seem like something that was necessary. I thought our communication was fine. I thought I was getting my point across and that I was understanding hers. After a few misunderstandings (which were usually my fault), I realized how extremely helpful feedback is to me.

However, getting feedback from Sue wasn't easy at first. I remember feeling uncomfortable and a bit awkward, but I realized that my words weren't as clear as I thought they were and that I needed to improve on what I was saying and how I said it (my tone). With Sue and I working together on communication in our marriage, we noticed improvements in every area of our lives.

Now, feedback is something that I welcome in all of my relationships. I don't feel uncomfortable or awkward, but rather I look forward to giving and receiving feedback. It roots out miscommunication and makes way for an open and honest relationship. I want to be understood, and I want to understand what is said to me. Communicating about what was said, heard, and meant has made life good. Feedback is what has made the difference.

HONESTY

It's one thing to master talking, listening, and giving feedback. It's another to be honest with your spouse.

Many times, we think that our lies don't matter. They seem harmless enough—we aren't trying to hurt anyone—and so we let it slide. But in any relationship, you can't live with deceitful lies and expect to maintain a strong, healthy marriage with the anchor line of communication.

Early in my marriage, I found myself lying by default. It didn't seem like a big deal at the time because I wasn't trying to deceive Sue. I wasn't being malicious or cunning. I was protecting her and myself (or so I thought). I loved God and Sue with all my heart, but I was lying to keep the peace, to avoid drama, and to preserve the relationship and not to ruffle feathers. I feared being rejected, misunderstood, or falsely judged if I told the truth, so I lied by default. I know as a reader you must be judging me right now, and I get it (sow mercy, my friends).

You've never been dishonest when asked, "Does this dress make me look fat?" or "How's the meal?" when you know how long your wife took to prepare the meal. Maybe you've never caved when asked, "Would you like to go shopping?"

You probably responded, "Yeah, that was at the top of the list today, just above hunting or fishing." And women, what about when you've been asked, "How much did that dress and new pair of shoes cost?" or "Did we really need those new curtains?" I know you've never been tempted to lie when asked, "Do you still have a headache?"

Even in ministry, you can be tempted to lie when asked, "Do you remember me?" or "Did you pray for me this week, Pastor?" You just don't want the drama or hurt feelings by telling the truth. You hate to say, "No, I haven't prayed for you, I've been shopping with my wife instead of hunting or fishing"—let it go!—"or praying."

The Lord showed me what I was doing. Through His grace and mercy, He helped me with my problem, and I determined never to lie by default again. I chose truth and honesty, and it's been a game changer in my life. I sleep at night. I don't have any of the nagging feelings you get when you've told a lie. I feel free, without baggage.

We may think that by lying, we're protecting the person we love. We don't want their feelings to get hurt or for them to know the reality of what's going on in life. And yet by choosing to lie, we make it worse.

When you figure out how to speak the truth in love, you will grow *"in every way more and more like Christ"* (Ephesians 4:15 NLT). Truth and truth spoken in love is essential to build and grow a healthy relationship. You and your spouse must learn to be honest in every situation, circumstance, and conversation, even when it's difficult or unpleasant. I'm not suggesting we be mean and hurtful, cloaked and masked, "in the name of truth." Too many people today love to speak truth but are mean and hurtful about it. We need to speak the truth in love with as much grace and mercy as possible.

You must be committed to honesty, or you're never going to make it. It's as simple as that. There are three key solutions for developing honesty in your marriage relationship and beyond.

First, reward honesty. When the truth is unpleasant, our tendency is to punish the person who spoke it. However, by doing this, we tell our spouse that we don't want them to be honest. We don't want the truth. Having a loving and grateful response—even when the truth hurts—will encourage a habit of honesty. Never reward lying by punishing the truth.

Second, value the truth in what's being said. As you communicate more with one another, you will learn to see and value its worth. You will find freedom in being honest with one another. Truth brings freedom and lies enslave (John 8:31-32).

Third, seek God together. He is the great Healer. He will bring emotional health as you develop honesty and strengthen the lines of communication within your marriage.

If Sue asks me, "Does this dress make me look fat?" I can respond in honesty, "Do I look stupid?" *Let it go!*

ANCHOR LINE 2

Communication

Communication is hard. Choosing to listen closely, hear clearly, and understand well takes dedicated work. There will be setbacks, but know that if you mess up, you have the option of asking for forgiveness and pushing the restart button to begin the next day with new understanding. Together, with your spouse, you can build the anchor line of healthy communication as you seek to keep God at the center of your marriage.

WORKBOOK

Chapter Two Questions

Question: Describe the differences between how you communicate and how your spouse communicates, including your reasons, motivations, and preferences for talking. How can understanding those differences help you communicate more effectively with each other?

Question: Have you fallen into a habit of using harsh words, hurtful sarcasm, or know-it-all interruptions when communicating with your spouse? How do these hurt your marriage?

Are you honest in your communication? Have you ever withheld information from your spouse "to protect them," though you were really only protecting yourself?

Question: How would your spouse describe the way you listen to him or her? Do you make a choice to set aside distractions and focus on your spouse? Do you make an effort to understand what is being said even when you (think you) disagree? Do you provide appropriate feedback to clarify and make sure you truly heard and understood?

Action: Plan a date night centered around communication. Go somewhere that will provide a quiet atmosphere with few distractions. Ahead of time, prepare a list of conversation-starting questions (a quick Internet search for "date night questions" yields multiple choices). Take turns answering questions and intentionally listening to each other. Remember, the goal is not to check all the questions off the list, but to practice your communication skills.

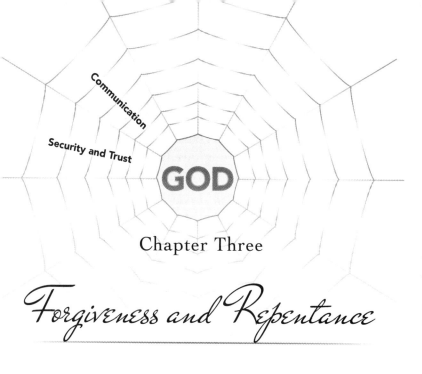

Communication

Security and Trust

GOD

Chapter Three

Forgiveness and Repentance

One of the ways we prove love for one another is by forgiving each other. Forgiveness is a choice we make and an action we take to repair the damage that a wrongdoing has caused. It is a way to show just how much we love the person who has wronged us, for love *"keeps no record of wrongs"* (1 Corinthians 13:5 NIV). It's a way for us to say, "You are more important than what you did or what you said. I choose *you* over bitterness, anger, and resentment."

Asking for forgiveness, in complete humility, is more important than pride or being right.

In 2 Corinthians 2:9–11, Paul writes to the church at Corinth about forgiveness. He challenges them to be obedient in everything and to forgive because *"if indeed I have forgiven anything, I have forgiven that one for your sakes in the presence of Christ, lest Satan should take advantage of us; for we are not ignorant of his devices."* We should forgive quickly and wholeheartedly—not only because Christ has forgiven us, but because satan takes advantage of the situation when we don't forgive.

So many problems or offenses that crop up in marriages end up going unresolved for years. Just think about that. Husbands and wives hold on to their anger and resentment and pride, and they end up making room for the enemy to move in and do his thing.

The effects and consequences of an unforgiving spirit are real and happen in our marriages and families way too much. *We must learn how to forgive*, for if we don't, we risk everything. James 3:16 says, *"For where envying and strife is, there is confusion and every evil work"* (KJV). Strife is contention and selfish ambition as well as discord and division. Proverbs 13:10 says, *"Only by pride cometh contention"* (KJV). Unforgiveness is a form of pride that leads to our demise and, far too often, to the collapse of our marriages.

Humility is the opposite of pride. Humility repents and asks for forgiveness, and it also forgives. Pride never asks for or gives forgiveness. The symptoms of our pride and contention can range from screaming and hollering or throwing of pots and pans to the silent treatment. It's storming out of a room. It's focusing on yourself when Jesus has called us to focus on Him and others.

These things allow satan to *steal, kill, and destroy* your marriage (John 10:10). We must be quick to repent when we make *mistakes, and we should be quick to forgive* when our spouse or children make mistakes. It's truly amazing what happens when we simply say, "I'm sorry," "I was wrong." The simple choice to forgive in those moments is profound.

THE PROCESS OF FORGIVENESS

Many people believe forgiveness is an emotion, and it can be. But ultimately, forgiveness is a choice. You might be hurt because of what someone has done or said to you. You may feel broken inside, with your emotions all over the place, but you can choose forgiveness. Even when you don't feel like it, you can choose the right path. It's only when you choose to forgive that God can come in and heal you from your pain. Healed emotions are the by-product of forgiveness, not the action of forgiveness. They are the fruit of forgiveness, not the root.

Let me quickly cover what forgiveness is not because so many people are confused and think they just *can't* forgive certain people or offenses. Forgiving is not forgetting, as so many have been taught. Some things have happened to many of us that cannot be forgotten, but you can still forgive. You probably will not be able to forget you've been divorced or molested as a child (nor should you), but you can forgive and be released of the pain and torment. Forgiveness is not trust. Forgiveness is a gift because of God's love being extended. Trust, by definition, has to be earned. I've forgiven people of hurts and wrongdoing, but trust can only be built when there is fruit of repentance. You can forgive an uncle of molesting you as a child, but I recommend you not forget or trust him around your children. If repentance and fruits of repentance have occurred, restoration becomes possible, but blind trust is not good. I have other teachings online if you would like to learn more on this subject.

WHAT IS FORGIVENESS?

- Forgiveness is releasing someone from a debt.
- Forgiveness is settling the amount owed.
- Forgiveness is patching mistreatment when possible.

- Forgiveness is righting the wrong when allowed.

It does not harbor bitterness against someone's actions. It doesn't hold on to the past. It seeks restitution. It releases the other person (your spouse) from debt.

Matthew 18:21–35 tells about a man who owed the king a great debt. The king was about to sell all that the man owned to pay the debt. When the man threw himself at the king's feet and begged for mercy, the king took pity upon the man and erased his debt completely. The man then went home and found a servant who owed him a small bit of money. Instead of showing the servant the same mercy that had just been shown to him, the man threw the servant into debtor's prison. When the king heard of this, he was furious:

> *Then the master called the servant in. "You wicked servant," he said, "I canceled all that debt of yours because you begged me to. Shouldn't you have had mercy on your fellow servant just as I had on you?" In anger his master handed him over to the jailers to be tortured, until he should pay back all he owed.*
>
> *This is how my heavenly Father will treat each of you unless you forgive your brother or sister from your heart* (Matthew 18:32–35 NIV).

Jesus wants us to forgive each other. He wants us to cancel debts and free people from their transgressions against us. He wants us to let God be the ultimate judge. Matthew 6:9–13 is commonly known as the Lord's Prayer. Part of that prayer, in verse 12, calls us to declare that God would *"forgive us our debts, as we forgive our debtors."* Forgiveness simply releases debt, and people, to God's righteous judgment. No one gets away with anything in the eyes of the Lord. Forgiveness is releasing people of any debt but trusting God to righteously judge, if not in this life then in the life to come. Forgiveness releases others to God and His righteous judgment and allows God to heal my emotions and releases me from any tormentors. Many falsely believe the torment they experience is because of what was done to them instead of their unforgiveness being the cause. Unforgiveness leads to torment, not what was done to me. Forgiveness releases me from torment and who hurt me to God.

FORGIVENESS IN MARRIAGE

The Bible speaks of darkness in three major categories—sin, trespasses, and iniquities. All three of these affect marriages in different ways. While all sin is equally bad to God (there are no good sins), not all sin is equal. There are variations in consequences of sins. While lying and murder are equally wrong and sinful, they are not equal in consequences. Which would you prefer to be done to you? Stealing and adultery are equally wrong and sinful, but not equal. If you steal from me, you can pay restitution. How do you pay back for adultery?

Sin deliberately violates God's moral law. It's a transgression of God's divine law. We fall short of the glory of God when we break God's divine law (Romans 3:23). When we sin in marriage, repentance and forgiveness need to be the course of action. Iniquities are immoral acts that are evil or abominations in nature and done with malice and intent to harm. They are gross injustices or wickedness. In some cases, these occur in marriage and must be addressed and dealt with as well.

Most common, however, are trespasses, which can be dangerous as well. Matthew 6:14 says, *"For if you forgive men their trespasses, your heavenly Father will also forgive you."* In this verse, the Greek word used for trespasses is *paraptoma,* which means a "a side-slip (lapse or deviation), i.e., (unintentional) error or (willful) transgression" (Strong's #G3900).

A trespass can be an offense by accident. You did not mean to hurt or harm, but you did. Man, this is where I stumbled the most. There were times when I said something that I did not mean the way it came out or that I forgot something important, like an anniversary or a birthday.

A young newlywed man asked me how to remember his anniversary. I responded, "Just forget one time." Am I the only one to forget to pick up the kids or take out the trash? Am I the only one who couldn't remember that dinner was at 5 p.m.? Can anyone say "trespass"? I've unintentionally trespassed on private property in the past. Notice the signs say, "No trespassing," not "no sinning or iniquities." Believe it or not, there is a difference.

I think about American football when I think about trespasses in marriage. In every football play, when the teams line up to face off, there is an imaginary line that runs between them. The offense has ownership of one side of the line, and the defense has ownership of the other. When a defensive lineman crosses that imaginary line, the referee makes a signal and calls "encroachment," and it's a five-yard penalty. The player didn't intend or plan to cross the line, but to cross it is to be trespassing on the offence's property. A player's team members certainly won't hold it against him, but there are consequences for breaking the rules. They also prefer he not do it again or plan on doing it. If repeated enough, it could cost them the game.

The same is true for trespasses between spouses. Each spouse's opinions and thoughts or feelings are a part of their personal property, as is their way of doing things. The thing with trespasses is that if couples are unwilling to communicate through hard things on a daily basis, issues pile up. Encroachment happens time and again. Years pass, and before you know it, you and your spouse have a mountain of trespasses separating the two of you. The seemingly small penalty has accumulated, threatening the future of the marriage.

Each person must learn to forgive the offense and learn to let go. It's not the big things, like sins and iniquities, that destroy most marriages, but the building up of little things (trespasses). Solomon declared in Song of Solomon 2:15 that it was *"the little foxes that spoil the vineyards"* (ESV). Don't misunderstand—big things can ruin a marriage, but I submit to you it's the little things unresolved that ruin most marriages. The trespasses and encroachments are what can wear a spouse down. Be quick to repent and swift to forgive. Communicate the little things annoying or irritating you, if you can't just let it go (Proverbs 19:11). We should be able to just let the little encroachment go, but if you can't, discuss it (1 Peter 4:8; Proverbs 10:12).

ANCHOR LINE 3

Forgiveness and Repentance

> *Love is patient and kind. Love is not jealous or boastful or proud or rude. It does not demand its own way. It is not irritable, and it keeps no record of being wronged. It does not rejoice about injustice but rejoices whenever the truth wins out. Love never gives up, never loses faith, is always hopeful, and endures through every circumstance* (1 Corinthians 13:4–7 NLT).

First Peter 4:8 says we are to cultivate a loving relationship with our spouse: *"Above all things have intense and unfailing love for one another, for love covers a multitude of sins [forgives and disregards the offenses of others]"* (AMPC). Peter's intention here isn't to imply that love participates in a cover-up of sin. Rather, he suggests that we should seek to restore, not destroy, the person who committed the offense.

In marriage, we commit offenses innocently. We trespass and get under one another's skin, and we don't mean to do it—we don't mean to hurt or frustrate one another. But the trespasses pile up, time begins to pass, and suddenly the person you love the most has become the person you like the least. The only way to move forward in a healthy way is to ask for and offer forgiveness.

The anchor line of forgiveness and repentance calls us to give one another the benefit of the doubt, to hold off on judgment but be quick to forgive. The One who sees all, who hears all, who knows all is right there with you, cheering you on.

The Lord promised to be with us and never leave or forsake us. Forgiveness and repentance issues can be hard to discuss with your spouse. However, as you each dedicate yourselves to saving and restoring the marriage by forgiving each other's trespasses, you will grow in your marriage relationship. And through communicating those differences, you can turn the tide of darkness and destruction and strengthen this third anchor line toward a healthy marriage.

WORKBOOK

Chapter Three Questions

Question: How should the offended party in a marriage confront in love when the other spouse does not appear repentant or has not sought forgiveness? Why is loving confrontation so important (Matthew 18:15)? Conversely, are there times when it is right to just let something go (Proverbs 19:11)? How do you know the difference?

Question: What is the source of torment in our lives—what was done to us or unforgiveness?

Question: Have you ever refused to forgive your spouse for something? What was the impact on you personally as well as on your marriage? Why is unforgiveness such a trap?

Question: What is forgiveness? What is forgiveness *not*?

Question: When there has been a break of fellowship in your marriage, are you quick to ask for forgiveness, or do you stubbornly wait for your spouse to "give in" first, assuming their share of the blame is larger? How could it change the dynamics in your relationship if you consistently took the initiative to make things right and to seek and offer forgiveness?

Action: Individually, in a time of prayer and/or journaling, spend some time reflecting on the ways that God has forgiven and restored you. Then ask Him to give you His forgiveness toward your spouse and His perspective on them.

Action step: What could you ask for forgiveness for?

Forgiveness and Repentance

Communication

Security and Trust

GOD

Chapter Four

Finances

Each person handles money differently. Some view money as an investment, a way to build wealth. Others view money as a tool, a means to help others. And still others view money as a luxury, something that can make life easier. Chances are, you and your spouse each have a unique and differing view of money—and chances are, it's caused more than a few arguments in the past. While Sue and I have never argued over money, we have had to navigate through differences and rather arduous discussions and debates (okay, we argued!).

Money talks a lot, and how you handle your money says a lot about you and your life. Jesus taught in Matthew that *"where your treasure is, there your heart will be also"* (Matthew 6:21 NIV). So we know from Scripture that there is a delicate balance and connection between money and the condition of our hearts. All you have to do is look at where the money goes and you'll know where the heart is. "Show me the money" and I'll "show you the heart."

This is why Scripture teaches so much about stewardship and finances. Money has a profound effect on the heart. It can turn someone toward God just as easily as it can turn someone away from God. This is why the anchor line of finances is so very important in your marriage relationship. As you seek God together and direct your heart to Him, you will find that He might change the way you view your finances.

As I've stated earlier, this subject requires hours and hours of searching the Scriptures and learning to trust God with your finances. Scripture teaches us that finances are not just natural, but very spiritual (Luke 16 and 19). Faithfulness with money is a test that affects other areas of our lives. Nothing stirs people up for or against God more than money.

In Luke 16:10, Jesus said, *"If you are faithful in little things, you will be faithful in large ones. But if you are dishonest in little things, you won't be honest with greater responsibilities"* (NLT). He was talking about handling money and stewardship. He called that a little thing, but to most individuals it's the biggest. If we can't handle money and the temptations that come with money, how will we ever handle the true riches of the Kingdom? Let me just cover some simple basics, but I encourage you as a couple to spend a lifetime growing in wisdom concerning finances.

CREATING AND MAINTAINING A BUDGET

Just as there are differing views on money, there are differing views on budgets. Many people may think they don't need a budget, while others scrutinize and itemize down to the penny. The Bible, however, teaches that God wants us to be responsible with our money but not be ruled by it (Ecclesiastes 5:10; Luke 14:13–14; 1 Timothy 5:8; 1 Timothy 6:10; Hebrews 13:5; Proverbs 13:11, 22). Achieving this balance is crucial to having a healthy relationship with God and money.

While there are diverse types of budgets and hundreds of approaches to handling money, there are a few rules that I have found to be universally true if you're going to have a healthy relationship with money:

1.   Give God His share (10 percent).
2.   Live below your means (80 percent).

3. Save and invest the rest (10 percent).

Tithing simply means 10 percent of your income. Tithing is an important part of the anchor line of finances. Many feel they can't afford to tithe. It's something that you can't afford not to do! When you tithe, you are engaging with God on a whole new level. You are saying, "I trust You so much with every facet of my life, I'm giving back to You what You've given me." Tithing is a way for you and your spouse to look to God to meet all your needs according to His riches and glory—not according to your paycheck. Tithing releases supernatural income and influence in the Kingdom of God.

So with that hundred dollars that God gives you, give ten percent back to Him. Give it to your church, where you are led and fed. Invest in the God who is investing in you.

Tithing is not an old covenant law but was established by Abraham, hundreds of years before the law. I have other teachings on this that are available for free online. Abraham tithed to Melchizedek; Isaac also tithed, as did many others. Tithing was practiced before the law, under the law, and still continues after the law. Sue and I give much more than 10 percent, but that's a good start. It's the first thing we do with any increase of income or our weekly compensation. Living on the 90 percent with God's blessing and help is smarter than living on 100 percent without God's blessing associated with tithing.

> *Honor the Lord with your possessions, and with the firstfruits of all your increase; So, your barns will be filled with plenty, and your vats will overflow with new wine* (Proverbs 3:9-10).

Firstfruits are a direct reference to tithing, and notice the blessings that flow out of your faith obedience. Barns filled with plenty and vats overflowing with new wine was a way of saying "blessed with plenty."

Live Below Your Means

Too many people live above their means, which puts unnecessary stress on a marriage. If one hundred dollars a week comes in, you don't need more than eighty going out. But if a hundred dollars a week is coming in with 120 dollars going out, then you know you're in trouble. In fact, if you keep it up, you'll be in trouble the rest of your life.

The bottom line is that if God has given you one hundred dollars, He expects you to live within those means. If you can't handle the hundred dollars, you won't be able to handle a thousand dollars or ten thousand dollars. To develop and maintain a healthy relationship in your marriage, it's important to not allow money to become a trouble area. Live within your means, get on the same page with your spouse when it comes to budgeting and spending, and trust God with the rest.

You cannot spend money you do not have and have a stress-free marriage. Your basic needs and enjoyment, entertainment, eating out, hobbies, giving to others should not exceed 80 percent. Food (weekly supply), shelter (place to live), and mobility (car, etc.) would obviously fall under the 80 percent as well as clothes. These hard costs can change as God blesses your stewardship in your finances. The car and home Sue and I have today far exceed what we had when first married. Our 80 percent has increased, but we still live under our means. Remember, just because there are checks in the checkbook or a debit card in your wallet doesn't mean there is money in the bank. Credit cards, if paid off monthly, can be a convenience and blessing, but if there is no discipline, they lead to ruin. If you can't say no to spending, then say yes to plastic surgery. (*Cut the card up*, if you missed that one!).

Save and Invest the Rest—10 percent

What happens with the last ten percent of your earnings? Remember, eighty percent goes to meet your needs, wants, and offerings; ten percent goes to your church; and ten percent is left over. You and your spouse should set the remaining ten percent aside as savings or investments for your future.

Today's culture does not see the need to save up and invest in the future. We live in the moment. We want things now. The thought of putting money away and not touching it for years and years is almost a foreign concept. But if you have the discipline of saving money, when investment opportunities come, you will be able to invest and position yourself to reap a harvest. Furthermore, you'll prevent marital strain. When those unexpected bills come, you'll have a backup plan.

COMMUNICATING ABOUT DEBT

Debt is not a black-and-white issue. It's not always wrong or always right, and it certainly isn't a sin. But it can cause a lot of strife in marriage if you and your spouse have differing views on how to handle it. It can become a sin if not paid off.

The culture we live in encourages debt. We spend money we don't have just to secure immediate gratification or just to have a slightly better car, house, phone, or outfit. And then the bills come, and the stress hits.

Just as today's culture leverages credit and debt to its advantage, so you need to learn to leverage credit and debt to *your* advantage. Credit card machines at checkout counters don't mean you always have to reach for your card. The sooner you and your spouse can come to a healthy understanding of debt (good debt versus bad debt), the less debt you'll accumulate, the fewer bills you'll have to pay, and the less pain you'll suffer in your marriage.

The story of Elisha and the widow in 2 Kings 4:1–7 illustrates the good and bad of debt. It tells the story of a widow who was in debt after her husband died. Creditors came to collect their due, and all they could find worth taking were her sons.

The cultural system in those days viewed people as collateral. If a household got into too much debt, its sons and daughters would be taken and turned into bond servants or debt slaves. They had to work for the creditors until the debt was paid off.

The widow was deep in her grief. She had just lost her husband and now she was about to lose her boys.

When Elisha came to help her, all she had was a little oil in one pot. So Elisha told her, *"Go, borrow vessels from everywhere, from all your neighbors—empty vessels; do not gather just a few"* (2 Kings 4:3). Then he told her to pour the oil she had into each pot. By faith, she poured a little into the first pot and discovered more oil, so she kept pouring and pouring and filled up the pot. She continued this, filling up the second pot and the third. Soon, all the pots were filled. She sold the oil, paid the creditors off, and secured her two sons. Based on the usage of the word *borrow,* we can infer that she returned the pots to her neighbors once she sold the oil.

It's a beautiful story about how borrowing can do a lot of good. After all, she borrowed the pots and a miracle happened! But the story also implies she was able to return the pots to their owners. I'd like to think God wants our relationship with debt to be similar. We borrow only what is necessary, and we return it as soon as we can. I also like to think about the friends and neighbors around her who were happy to lend her their pots, helping her in a small way to secure her family unit.

Jesus taught about lending in Matthew 5:42 and Luke 6:34–36, and He was clear: If we are able to help a brother out, then we should do so. It is a blessing to lend to someone in need—expecting nothing in return—and, oftentimes, it points to a person's walk with God.

LEARN TO BE CONTENT

I grew up in poverty and saw the pain and strain it causes. But for all the trouble and strife it brought, poverty forced me to be content with what I had—and that's a lesson that I wouldn't trade for anything.

Whether you were raised in poverty or with affluence, contentment is the goal. As Paul wrote, *"Not that I speak in regard to need, for I have learned in whatever state I am, to be content: I know how to be abased, and I know how to abound"* (Philippians 4:11–12). To develop a healthy marriage, you must learn to be content with what God has given you. You must be thankful for His blessing, whether He gives you a hundred dollars or a million dollars. Millionaires need to be on a budget and should not spend what they don't have, either.

Contentment forces us to ignore the yearnings of the flesh. It forces us to discipline our desires, for our flesh to be reckoned dead—and that's a process. We may want, but we must learn to never demand and never expect to get what we want instantly. While foreign to many, delayed gratification is a healthy discipline.

This idea of being content and not getting things *now* may be difficult for you or your spouse. You might be forty years old and yet, when you're told "no," your immediate reaction is to throw a tantrum like a kid who isn't getting what he wants from the toy aisle! This is because no one loved you enough to teach you to discipline your flesh and say, "No, not now." No one showed you that if you can't be at peace without the thing you want, then you won't be at peace *with* it.

In 1 Timothy, Paul told Timothy, a young pastor, to avoid the trappings that come with being in the ministry. Paul says:

> *Now godliness with contentment is great gain. For we brought nothing into this world, and it is certain we can carry nothing out. And having food and clothing, with these we shall be content. But those who desire to be rich fall into temptation and a snare, and into many foolish and harmful lusts which drown men in destruction and perdition. For the love of money is a root of all kinds of evil, for which some have strayed from the faith in their greediness, and pierced themselves through with many sorrows* (1 Timothy 6:6–10).

As Paul says, we brought nothing into this world, and it's certain we will carry nothing out when we die. We should be content with the food and clothing God has given us.

It's important to note that Paul isn't saying we can't have more than that—and he isn't saying we shouldn't *believe* that we can receive more than that. Essentially—and this is key here—Paul is saying we must learn to be content and live with what we already have. Getting more won't make us happier if we aren't happy with what we have now.

To sustain a marriage relationship (and every other relationship, for that matter), we must recognize the need for God to be at the forefront of everything we do, including how we manage our finances. We need this anchor line, or we risk allowing money, possessions, and greed to get the better of us. God is the foundation for everything we do in our marriages, and being good stewards of what He has given us is paramount to strengthening this anchor line in our marriage relationship.

ANCHOR LINE 4

Finances

Proverbs 3:16 tells us that wisdom has two hands. In her right hand is *"length of days,"* and in her left hand she holds *"riches and honor."* Ultimately, your wealth comes from wisdom and not from your employer alone. Wisdom, we know, comes from God. Once we recognize this, we will see how He blesses us beyond our paycheck.

When I was a young adult, I didn't understand passive income. I thought it meant you stayed in bed all day and money fell from the sky (No, really, I did!). In reality, though, a passive income is when your money works for you instead of you working for your money. It multiplies and grows and brings more wealth—all on its own. Passive income is God's desire for all of us. It's His will of basic stewardship. He wants us to sit back and trust Him, believe Him, as He pours wisdom over us—wisdom in finances, wisdom in relationship, wisdom in life. But we must prove ourselves worthy and faithful.

Jesus observes that if we can't be wise stewards who are faithful with a little, we won't be able to handle the "true riches" of life that God wants to bestow upon us (Luke 16:8–14). To have a proper perspective with money, you must be faithful with a little. This means making sure to have healthy discussions with your spouse regarding budgeting, values, and stewardship of your finances.

WORKBOOK

Chapter Four Questions

Question: How do you view money? How does your spouse view it? What are your differing values when it comes to money? A fun way to understand this is to ask each other what you would do with an unexpected $100, $1,000, and $10,000.

Question: If you feel compelled to tithe or give in a specific way but your spouse does not, how can you get on the same page?

Question: Has debt been a servant to you, or have you been a slave to debt? How can you work together to move your debt from a burden to a tool and then finally to unnecessary?

Action: In what areas do each of you struggle with contentment? Do you have different financial backgrounds that have led to differing expectations about money? Together, write out your needs and your wants. Come up with a plan to meet the needs and save toward the wants. Read a book or attend a class on biblical money management to help with creating a budget and setting mutual short- and long-term goals for your money.

Forgiveness and Repentance

Finances

Communication

Security and Trust

GOD

Chapter Five

Roles and Responsibilities

Our entire culture is collapsing over the roles and responsibilities of husband and wife. The moment you mention the topic, even at church, there's pushback. We live in a society that has absolutely resisted everything God says about marriage. There is not only resistance to God and His Word, but there is also rebellion and offense toward God.

We argue over the role of the man and the role of the woman, and we struggle to find any sort of common ground. And all the while, basic needs within the marriage go unmet and couples become needless causalities of divorce. The anchor line of roles and responsibilities helps couples to shore up and strengthen this very important area, seeing to it that needs are met while at the same time everyone is valued and loved.

THE CHRISTLIKE MARRIAGE

Ephesians 5 addresses the Spirit-filled life. Verses 22–28 talk specifically about wives submitting to their husbands and about husbands loving their wives as Christ loved the church. The following verses break down the roles of the husband and wife, with the husband as a picture of Jesus and the wife a picture of the church.

The takeaway is that marriage is holy. It is near and dear to God's heart because it symbolizes the relationship between Christ and the church. The marriage relationship is something we can see, but at the same time, as part of God's perfect plan for creation, it reveals something we cannot see—the relationship we have with Jesus. He has joined Himself to us in a covenant similar to a marriage covenant. In this, we are no longer two; we are one spirit in the Lord (1 Corinthians 6:17).

In Ephesians 5:32–33, God speaks to the key need a husband has and the key need a wife has. He says, *"This is a great mystery, but I speak concerning Christ and the church.*

Nevertheless let each one of you in particular so love his own wife as himself, and let the wife see that she respects her husband." For the husband, the need is respect. For the wife, the need is love. But simply meeting these needs is not enough. When each person's needs are also aligned with a strong, healthy relationship with God, then everything else in that marriage relationship will fall into place.

Men need to learn what it means to love their wives just as much as they love themselves. Women need to learn what it means to respect their husbands. Both must learn to love *and* respect God. Only with God's help can a husband love a wife as Christ loves the church. Likewise, it is only with God's help that a wife can respect a husband as the church does Jesus. Do these simple things, and you'll have a happy marriage.

MEETING NEEDS

It's interesting how God knows us so well, isn't it? Ephesians 5:28–29 commands husbands to love their wives just as they love their own bodies, that they are to nourish and cherish their wives (ESV). According to *Merriam-Webster*'s dictionary, to *nourish* is "to promote the growth of." To *cherish* is to "entertain or harbor in the mind deeply and resolutely." A husband is to be considering his wife and promoting and preferring her in their journey together in life.

The command for me to love seems to be a larger task than the command for Sue to respect. I'm not going to make a big deal out of submission (a form of respect). God knows how self-focused men can be! He knows that we think about *our* desires and needs first in many cases. And God knows that if we channel that love from ourselves to our wives, we'll be happily married.

For wives, He knows that if they show respect to their husband, they'll win him over and bring the best out of him. And if they show disrespect, they'll bring out the worst.

I've seen these truths play out numerous times. When a marriage is collapsing, I hear the husband say, "She loves me but does not respect me," while the wife says, "He respects me but doesn't love me." Both are upset. Both are hurt. And in most cases, both accusations are true.

The man is frustrated because he doesn't understand the kind of love that his wife desires. He thinks that going to work every day and coming home at night is showing love. She, however, wants more. She wants biblical love from him. She wants to be romanced, pursued, and nurtured. She wants to be his sole focus (second only to Jesus), his all, cherished by her husband.

On the flip side, the woman is frustrated. She doesn't understand how to show respect properly. She thinks that by cooking her husband a meal or asking for his opinion, she is showing respect. But he wants the biblical version of respect. He wants her to speak words of affirmation to him. He wants her to trust him even when she is unsure. He wants her to speak highly of him to others.

Men, love your wife with affection and romance.

Women, respect the role that God has given your husband to lead and oversee the home (Ephesians 5:23).

Do these things and watch God work in your marriage.

ROLES WITHIN MARRIAGE

So often we get caught up on who should do the dishes or who should discipline the children, but the core teaching behind marital roles is that husbands are to love their wives and wives are to respect their husbands.

"But how can this be? What about chores and responsibilities and dividing up the workload?" Let's look at both roles a little deeper and see how they apply in the marriage relationship.

Ephesians 5:23 says, *"For the husband is the head of the wife, even as Christ is the head of the church: and he is the saviour of the body"* (KJV). *Head* of the home does not mean *oppressor* of the home. It doesn't mean the husband should manipulate, control, or abuse his wife and children. Being the head is a very serious role commanded by God to lead the household heavenward.

Practically, this works out in many different ways, but the word *head* here simply means a *covering*, and it points to God's divine order in the marriage relationship. The husband is the covering of the wife and the home—and if you understand headship in the Bible, then you know just how positive this role is for all involved.

Scripture tells us the head of the woman is the man, the head of man is Christ, and the head of Christ is God (1 Corinthians 11:3). All of these are to emulate the Christ/Father God relationship. God is not abusive to the Son, nor is He manipulative or oppressive toward the Son. The Father and Son depict a beautiful relationship in which Jesus follows and trusts the Father while being loved and protected. Jesus submits to the Father.

That model should be displayed in our marriages as well. Jesus guides and directs the husband, who guides and directs his family. This is called divine order. This is how the anointing flows.

No man is the Savior (capital S) of any woman or anyone else, but they are meant to be the savior of the body (natural realm)—that is, its provider, protector, and deliverer. The word *saviour* (savior) in the King James Bible in Ephesians 5:23 is lowercased because, I believe, the translator properly recognized that in this instance, it was referring to salvation in the natural realm, which could be applied not only to Jesus as head of His church but also, by analogy, to the husband as head of his wife.

If the word *savior* were reserved exclusively for Jesus, we couldn't apply it to anyone else. However, other passages in the Bible use the word *savior* in connection to God as well as to people or to God using people to bring deliverance to others in a natural, physical sense. This means that while Jesus is the ultimate Savior of our souls, people can be a different kind of savior. Samson was a savior and Gideon as well. For instance, Nehemiah 9:27 says, *"And according to thy manifold mercies thou gavest them saviours, who saved them out of the hand of their enemies"* (KJV). Obviously, these saviors did not rescue Israel in a spiritual sense from her sins, but they were saviors from Israel's natural enemies.

The husband is the (lowercase s) savior of the wife, which means he is supposed to provide for his wife and children to meet all their needs—not only financial needs, but also their physical and emotional needs.

The Bible reveals this principle of headship in the Garden of Eden within the context of original sin (Genesis 3). Adam's real sin was not protecting his wife from her temptation. The New Testament reveals that Eve was deceived, and it holds Adam accountable for their sin (1 Timothy 2:14). In the Genesis account, God visited the garden, but instead of going to Eve, who had been the first to sin, He went to Adam. God identified Adam as the savior of the body, responsible for his family. God had created Adam to be the head of his home, yet he had failed.

Adam was standing right beside her when Eve made the terrible decision to listen to the serpent. This passage shows that the problem of man forsaking his God-given duties began all the way back in the Garden of Eden, and because of sin, we see men neglecting to lead even today.

HUSBANDS, LOVE YOUR WIVES

We need to see a movement within the church, within marriages, and within homes in which men act as men of valor again. We need men to stand up and fight for their marriages and fight for and protect their wives and children. We may not be at war every day with a natural enemy oppressing us, but as husbands we must take up spiritual arms every day regardless. We must defend our family and fight for our family against the demonic powers of the culture around us, against the lure of the world, and against anything that would ensnare our wife, our children, and our legacy.

We need a movement where men will stand up and be men again. We need husbands who grab hold and secure this anchor line of roles and responsibilities. We need a generation of God-fearing heads of the household, not a generation of wimps who would rather take a back seat on easy street and submit to political correctness. Let's get back to biblical correctness.

It's not right when men bail out of the family like we see happening today. It's not right that men leave their wives with the responsibility of providing for the family. A woman may work two or three jobs and still have to be a mom to three or four kids. It's not right that some people in our government are endorsing and exacerbating demographic changes in our society that undermine the place of a husband and dad. Kids need dads, and wives need husbands. God didn't will and plan for the mother to work multiple jobs and raise those kids alone.

We need dads dedicated to the family and the home. We need dads who are committed to helping raise the kids. We need husbands to love and support their wives unconditionally and selflessly. Protecting our wives and daughters from the abuse in our culture is a real battle. Protecting our children from sexual predators of all types is a battle. Protecting our children's moral innocence and true identity as boys and girls is a real battle. Protecting their minds from the corruption of sexual love is a real battle.

Welcome to the fight, gentlemen, the good fight of faith. Be the savior God has called and anointed you to be. Any domestic support and help around the house is a good thing, but nothing like protecting your family from demonic assault. Your home is your garden, and you need to love your wife by protecting and guarding your family as you would yourself.

WIVES, RESPECT YOUR HUSBANDS

If husbands are to selflessly love and lead their wives so that the anchor line of roles and responsibilities can be strengthened, then wives are to *"submit yourselves unto your own husbands, as unto the Lord"* (Ephesians 5:22 KJV). Aren't you thankful, ladies, that you don't have to submit to anyone else's husband?

When people hear the word *submission*, there can be panic. Because of sin, we are seeing a generation that doesn't want to submit to anyone anywhere. In the church, women can get offended because of the abuse and misuse of the word *submit*, and understandably so, but it needs to be fixed. We can't throw the baby out with the bath water by not gaining an understanding of the biblical meaning of submission. In the world, we see pushback from a culture that doesn't want to submit to teachers, police officers, employers, or anyone else. They don't want to be told what to do or instructed a certain way. All rules of civility are collapsing, and chaos is ensuing.

There's no way around submission in the workplace. The very act of going to work is an act of submission to your employer. It doesn't mean you are less than or under anyone's thumb. Rather, you have chosen to obey the requirements of your workplace. You've chosen to abide by their expectation that you show up. Submission is the glue to a healthy and moral society.

We must learn to submit like this in all places, but specifically for marriage. Submission means the wife is to follow the husband's lead unless it violates conscience or clear scriptural principles. In Scripture, we are taught to submit to civil authorities (Romans 13; 1 Peter 2). Peter submitted to civil authority until that authority violated God's authority. In Acts 4:18, authorities commanded Peter and John to not speak or teach in the name of Jesus. That command violated God's command to speak and teach in the name of Jesus throughout the world (Matthew 28:18–20; Mark 16:16–18).

Acts 4:12 says, *"There is no other name under heaven given among men by which we must be saved."* Peter and John were under no obligation to obey man, if that obedience required disobedience to God. They remained submissive to civil authorities but did not obey an ungodly command. After having been beaten, they did not leave that council and burn the town down. They left rejoicing, counting it an honor to suffer for Jesus' sake. *"Peter and the other apostles answered and said, 'We ought to obey God rather than men'"* (Acts 5:29).

In my book *Our Union with Christ*, I dedicate an entire chapter to submission in marriage and how it points to Christ our Husband. That chapter will thoroughly explain the difference between submission and obedience and when and how to not submit if you need further explanation.

It's important to note the difference between *submission* and *obedience*. Submission is an attitude. Obedience is the action. I have seen people who are submissive but didn't obey, and I've seen people who are obedient but not submissive.

In a marriage, a wife can have a submissive attitude and mindset while still choosing not to obey a directive that she feels is out of line. She can be calm, respectful, and communicative in a situation in which she has chosen not to obey. She is still submissive! She is still performing her role. But she is doing it with wisdom and discernment.

BEING A HELPMEET

In addition to respecting her husband and showing submission to him, the Bible also charges the woman to be a helpmeet for her husband. Genesis 2:18 says, *"And the Lord God said, It is not good that the man should be alone; I will make him an help meet for him*" (KJV). The word *helpmeet* is not to be confused with *helpmate!* The wife is not to be walked on and taken advantage of. But your husband is not a sinless man, and he doesn't live in a sinless world. He needs your help. Adam was sinless living in a sinless world and yet he needed help.

The New King James Bible refers to wives as "*homemakers*" (Titus 2:5). They are uniquely equipped to turn a house into a warm, inviting, nurturing space to raise a family. They know how to create refuge, safety, and peace within a living space. This doesn't mean they love to clean or cook or that they *enjoy* the day-to-day tasks that come with maintaining a home any more than we as husbands love everything at work outside the home. But it does mean that they bring something to a space that most men cannot. The woman domesticates a space, while most men need to be domesticated (by their wives)! I know Sue had to domesticate me.

Some people believe if a wife does anything outside the home, they've sinned against God, but that is not true. Women can work outside the home just as well as they can inside it. But it is important for a woman to understand her unique gifting within the home and for the man to support her in those. "Take out the trash" is not in the Bible, but I learned early it may fall under wisdom.

ANCHOR LINE 5

Roles and Responsibilities

The atmosphere of the home is powerful. From conversation at mealtime to bonding and raising children, the wife has the ability to influence the atmosphere, and the husband has the ability to lead it. *The Message* Bible translates it as *"keep a good house"* (Titus 2:5), and Ephesians 5:33 gives a charge to the husband and the wife:

> *However, let each man of you [without exception] love his wife as [being in a sense] his very own self; and let the wife see that she respects and reverences her husband [that she notices him, regards him, honors him, prefers him, venerates, and esteems him]* (AMPC).

This anchor line provides a healthy sense of each other's role and responsibilities in the marriage relationship. Through this, you and your spouse can love and respect and help each other, thereby strengthening your marriage and creating a peaceful atmosphere for whoever crosses the threshold of your door.

Support one another in serving the Lord. Bring love and respect into your marriage and help one another make the most of your unique gifting. That is God's best desire for this fifth anchor line.

WORKBOOK

Chapter Five Questions

Question: What does it mean for the husband to be the head of the home? What are his responsibilities? Why are so many men remiss in fulfilling this God-ordained role? How can the church encourage men to selflessly love, protect, and provide for their families?

Question: Define biblical submission. What is it, and what is it not? How does it fit in with the wife's responsibilities to respect her husband and be a helpmeet to him? Why is it so controversial in today's culture, and how can Bible believers talk about submission in a way that honors women and the biblical idea of marriage?

Question: Looking at these roles and responsibilities, how are you each doing? How can you support (not criticize) each other in fulfilling your biblical role? Pick one area you each can work on specifically over the next month. Plan ways to encourage your spouse when you see them working toward their goal.

Action: Wives, make a list for your husband: "I feel loved when…" Husbands, make a list for your wives: "I feel respected when…" Exchange lists. Commit to encouraging and thanking your spouse when they are intentional about fulfilling their role in a way that speaks to you.

Communication

Forgiveness and Repentance

Finances

Roles and Responsibilities

Security and Trust

GOD

Chapter Six

Sex and Romance

God created us as sensual beings. He created us to feel attracted to the opposite sex, to desire to be close to one another, and to respond positively to physical touch. And out of all of this, He created sex as the ultimate expression of sensuality and intimacy—as something that is very good between husband and wife.

The Church doesn't always teach it this way. If sex and sexuality are even mentioned at all, it's usually in the negative. All sex then is viewed as somehow impure. Even within marriage, it sometimes is considered to be a perversion deserving of God's judgment. But if Adam and Eve had sexual love before the fall—which we can infer from God's command to them to be fruitful and multiply (Genesis 1:28)—then sex in the marriage relationship has to be good. It has to be part of God's perfect plan for mankind.

God is the One who said they were to leave father and mother and cleave to each other (Genesis 2:24). One of the meanings of *cleave* is to have sex—to be glued together, figuratively speaking (Strong's #H1692). In Genesis 2:25, they were to celebrate and not be ashamed. There is definitely a need to get back to God's original plan! *Cleave* in the Hebrew means "to catch by pursuit." This one word covers the need of both husband and wife, sex and romance. I need to pursue Sue (romance), and she needs to let me catch her (sex). Amen!

We desperately need a healthy, godly perspective on sex and romance—it's why sex and romance is the sixth anchor line that we must secure within our marriages. Doing so will help us not just to be married but to be happily married. Romance is the atmosphere of the marriage; sex is the event and grand finale of romance.

GOD'S PLAN

In Genesis 2:18–24, God created a helpmeet for Adam. Because God couldn't find a helpmeet within the Garden for Adam, He took a rib from Adam's side and made a woman, Eve. The two were to have a unique and intimate relationship, and in this God designed marriage.

Because it was God who created marriage, He is the one who gets to dictate what it is or isn't. From Scripture, we know that marriage is two people, male and female, becoming one flesh, just as Adam and Eve were one, unified at the original creation. We know that marriage was ordained for us to make a lifelong covenant—not for us to live together for a time and "see how it goes." And marriage is for the purpose of cleaving to one another and becoming one flesh (Genesis 2:24).

So these are the things we know to be part of God's plan for sex and marriage. Yet so many relationships and marriages find themselves outside of His perfect plan.

Sex is a miracle from God; it joins two hearts and lives. But there are reasons why He placed sex within the boundary of marriage. Sex joins two people as one. Imagine what happens when you have multiple partners. Imagine taking that—taking them—into your marriage. Imagine the emotional damage. Imagine taking those memories, those experiences with you into the marriage bed. Or maybe you don't have to imagine; maybe you know firsthand what I'm talking about.

This is one reason why God hates divorce (Malachi 2:16). He hates what it does to people. It forces two people who have become one to pull apart. It's like trying to separate two sheets of paper that have been glued together. You can do it, but it's not going to be clean. You're bound to irreparably damage both sheets of paper. When individuals have sex with multiple partners, there is a gluing together and tearing apart that hurts and harms.

God knew all this when He created sex, and so that's why He intentionally placed it within the confines and safety of marriage. He knew that was the best, safest place for it. The *"flee fornication"* command in 1 Corinthians 6:18 (KJV) is for our protection and for the beauty of our sexuality within marriage. Hebrews 13:4 says, *"Marriage is honourable in all, and the bed undefiled"* (KJV). God sanctifies sexual relations in the institution of marriage, *"but whoremongers and adulterers God will judge"* (Hebrews 13:4b KJV). God warns us that He will judge those who defile the marriage bed by being given to sexual indulgence outside the boundaries of marriage.

So now that we know *why* God placed sex within marriage, how can you strengthen this anchor line? How can you make sure that this part of your marriage is as strong as it can possibly be? There are a few things that husbands need and a few things that wives need to feel fulfilled in this aspect of their marriage relationship.

DON'T FORGET ROMANCE

If you've ever been fishing, you may practice a catch-and-release policy. The idea is to release the fish back into the water so that you can catch them again. The same idea of pursuit should exist within the marriage relationship. Women need to be pursued and feel desired by their husband, and this happens through romance.

Romance is the atmosphere of the marriage, and a wife needs it to be alive and well to respond with loving openness to her husband. She needs consistent romantic experiences and expressions of her husband's love. She needs hugs, back rubs, kisses, and other physical gestures—and she needs them to be done without the goal of sex (she needs nonsexual hugs). I know, guys, just hold on.

Men often don't know what that means. A hug or kiss that doesn't go anywhere seems unnecessary! But many women desire emotional love more so than physical love. Women like candlelit dinners and romantic walks on the beach at sunset. They like to be romanced; they like to be wooed. Many men don't understand this. They want to jump right into bed and expect their wives to respond sexually when there has been no romantic buildup. This is where men and women are different. That's why this is so important to get right.

Husbands, tell your wife you love her—tell her every day. Do something thoughtful for her a few times a week. Hug without a motive. Kiss without a motive. Share your thoughts and heart with her. You don't need to understand it, but you do need to do it. Delayed gratification may be important here. This is a part of loving her the way she needs to be loved.

In response to this, one husband said, "I told her I loved her forty years ago, and if I change my mind, I'll tell her!" It's a response that might get a chuckle, but I fear that mindset is true for many men. They believe that by working hard and providing, they are showing their love. But women need to hear it! Men, how would you feel if your wife said, "I don't know what he needs sex for, we did that on our honeymoon," or "Sex, why? We already have all the kids we want."

The idea is the same here. We each have needs that only the spouse can provide, so we must take these roles very seriously. Your marriage depends on it.

FIVE APPROACHES OF ROMANCE

I struggled early in my marriage in the area of romance because I didn't have a good role model to teach me. I'd try to do this or that, and most of the time my efforts fell flat or turned into a crisis, not romance. I built a fireplace once, in our bedroom, and nearly burned the house down. I took Sue out on a boat ride across Lake Texoma, and we had a beautiful dinner by the water as we watched the sun go down. Because it was dark, I got lost and ran out of gas, and we were stranded on the lake until 4 a.m. Not too good. Yet, while romance wasn't necessarily the end result, Sue has always appreciated the effort.

Finally, I asked God to show me how to love Sue through romance, as well as help other husbands be a blessing to their wives. He revealed five important approaches that bring romance into the marriage relationship. Of course, Sue helped me as well.

1. *The unexpected.* Doing the unexpected can turn anything into a romantic gesture. You could stay home and spend time with your wife when she expected you to be out with friends. You could take her to dinner when she expected to cook a meal. You could ask her to watch the sunset with you on the lake (with a compass and map hidden in the boat of course). You could rise early to make breakfast. These are just a few of the many ways you can surprise your wife with your thoughtfulness. If I made breakfast, my wife would definitely be surprised and

hopefully be blessed by the effort (I'm praying over that one because I'm not sure it would be edible.).

2. *The impractical.* Young men instinctively understand romance, but as we get older and more comfortable in marriage, the romance starts to decline, and we become much too practical and mature in our approach to life. While maturity is a commendable character trait in a husband, it can be an enemy to romance. Similarly, practicality is an enemy of romance. Spend extra money on a nice dinner. Take that extra day off to be with her. Dare to be impractical and you'll find that she will respond. A motel for a getaway may be practical, but a five-star hotel is romantic. Sue is a different person when there is a number on the door!

3. *The creative.* Sometimes you have to think outside the box to really impress your wife. I remember a time in our marriage when I didn't have any money to buy something special for Sue, so I picked some wildflowers and made a little homemade card to say how much I loved her. I felt silly, but she teared up. That little creative gesture was not about the money, but about thinking of her and finding a way to show how much she meant to me. It was one of the few times my gesture didn't end up in disaste. (*Thank You, Jesus!*).

4. *Dating.* Planning a date can be a wonderful way to win over your lady's heart. Sue and I didn't date before we

got married—not in the traditional sense. But ever since our vows, we have made a point to go out together and have dates. It's not the food, but the fellowship that we look forward to the most, sharing things with each other and talking about the future. A date can help the two of you unwind and get back to the heart connection that brought you together in the first place. Even though dates are usually planned, the unexpected can always happen.

5. *Be gentle and kind.* When I'm really pressed for time or just don't know how to best show Sue my love, I bring it back to the fruit of the Spirit. Love, joy, peace, long-suffering, kindness, goodness, faithfulness, gentleness, self-control (Galatians 5:22–23)—these affect your marriage, and they are a guide to romance. Do something little that's kind, something that brings joy, and something that is gentle. These things will go a long way when it comes to making a mark on your wife's heart.

Romancing your wife is an element to a happy marriage, but sex is an element, too. And the Lord has plenty to say about it.

SANCTIFIED MARRIAGE

In Genesis, after the creation of mankind, God created marriage and defined it as a man leaving his parents and cleaving to his wife (Genesis 2:24). He created Adam and

Eve as sexual beings without shame—just think of that! Unfortunately, this concept is foreign to many Christians. Sex suffered as a result of the fall but didn't contribute to it, and like every beautiful thing that God gave us to enjoy, it became something He never intended it to be. God had created sex as a statement of Adam and Eve's perfection, not their perversion. Sadly, today we focus more on the perversion. We need to be reactivated from the Word of God and look back to what God intended sex to be.

Hebrews 13:4 says, *"Marriage is honorable among all, and the bed undefiled; but fornicators and adulterers God will judge."* This means that sex—within the confines of marriage—is pure and sanctified. God gave husbands and wives to enjoy each other sexually within the marriage relationship and to be faithful to each other.

This passage in Hebrews 13:4b doesn't mean that we can condemn others (or even ourselves) for wrongful actions. God is a God who forgives, but if people refuse and reject His gift of forgiveness, they will be righteously judged at the appearing and kingdom of Jesus. However, we also shouldn't condone things that hurt us and our families. Sexual perversion, sexual shaming, pornography and adultery—these are man-created extremes that are absolutely destructive to people and to marriages.

SEX IN ITS EXTREMES

One sexual extreme that we still battle today is the idea that it is necessary to refrain from sex in marriage in order to be pure and holy before God. Paul warned of this, saying:

> *The Spirit clearly says that in later times some will abandon the faith and follow deceiving spirits and things taught by demons. Such teachings come through hypocritical liars, whose consciences have been seared as with a hot iron. They forbid people to marry and order them to abstain from certain foods, which God created to be received with thanksgiving by those who believe and who know the truth* (1 Timothy 4:1–3 NIV).

This religious philosophy believes that, in order to be close to God, you need to remove sex. It says, "To be good with God is to refrain from sex." How sad!

Another extreme is the world's view that, in order to have great sex, you have to take God out of the equation—no rules, boundaries, or monogamous relations. This results in people viewing the Bible as some kind of oppressive, anti-sex book that wants us to stay sexually repressed. It has resulted in Hollywood and college campuses eliminating marriage from the sexual conversation.

Great colleges like Harvard and Yale were founded on Christian principles with the Bible as their primary textbook. They once believed that *"the fear of the Lord is the beginning of wisdom"* (Proverbs 9:10 KJV). But now, even talking too much about God or bringing Bible teaching into the classroom conversation can get you expelled or, at the very least, mocked and persecuted. Political correctness has replaced biblical correctness. There is a Bible phobia on many of our college campuses and in the media at large. Even "free speech" is forbidden if God, the Bible, or conservative values are expressed.

The Bible is clear on both of these extremes: We can be close to God *and* have great sex. We can avoid sexual perversions and be sexually fulfilled. It's not one or the other. With the anchor line of Sex and Romance secure, sex is even better when we have the Holy Spirit to guide us in our marriage relationship. Wives, share that with your husband, and they may want to be Spirit-filled.

A BALANCED VIEW

The biblical view of sex is clear, yet we've distorted it. We've included too many opinions and beliefs that may not align with what Scripture truly teaches. Let's look at the truth about sex and marriage.

Sex is not moral or immoral. It's *amoral*, which means that it can be used for good or bad purposes. There are many things in this life that are amoral, but like sex, we tend to view them one way or the other. Television, for example, was often classified as immoral, but it's what we allow to come across the television screen that is important and makes the difference. We can watch good things, or we can watch bad things. Television is not always good or always bad.

Money is another example of an amoral thing. Money is not inherently evil; it can be used in wonderful ways. Rather, the *love* of money is what we must look out for and avoid. It's the love of money that drives greed, causing us to never be satisfied with what we have. So money in itself is amoral because it can be used for good or bad purposes.

Something that is amoral needs good, strong boundaries. Like fire and water, sex is good within its God-given boundaries, but outside those boundaries, it can be damaging. Fire inside the fireplace is warm, but when it breaks outside the boundaries, it's dangerous. It's the same thing with water. Water nourishes the earth, and yet flooding, hurricanes, tsunamis are extremely dangerous and life-threatening. Water within the banks of a river is life to a city. Outside the banks due to floods, it can wipe out an entire town. We can live three to four days without water, but only a minute or so under it.

These two elements—fire and water—have the potential to destroy what's around them just as easily as they have the potential to help what's around them. Because of our culture's view on sex and marriage, the challenge for churches and parents is in explaining to our young people how God views sex as being beautiful within its boundaries of marriage between a man and woman. We need to enjoy sexual love in marriage.

To God, there's no such thing as casual sex. A powerful and mystical union from God happens in sexual love, and the power of it diminishes through having multiple partners. "Safe sex" is defined in Scripture as a husband and a wife in union with one another. It's not only safe, it's a lot of fun!

First Corinthians 6:12–20 says that our bodies are parts of Christ, and what we do with our bodies matters because a person joined to the Lord is one spirit with Him. There's something holy about sex that points to our rebirth as Christians and our relationship with Jesus. And just as our body is the temple of the Holy Spirit, sexual immorality and sexual perversion are sins against our own bodies (1 Corinthians 6:18). And I'm not sure we grasp the gravity of that truth.

When we knowingly sin, we do so because we think we can manage the consequences by either avoiding or predicting them. We choose to have an intimate dating relationship because we assume we'll get married anyway. We choose to look at pornography because we assume no one will find out. We choose to commit adultery because we think we can juggle a double life.

But the consequences that we foresee do not usually play out in the same way. The person we were intimate with chooses not to marry us, and the brokenness is deeper and more damaging than predicted or conceived. The pornography that we sneak soon becomes an addiction that is wreaking havoc. The adulterous relationship ends up destroying our marriage and harming so many others around us.

There are always consequences for believers and unbelievers. Sometimes, the consequences are spiritual, and they push us away from God. Satan condemns us and guilts us into believing God is mad at us or doesn't love us any longer. Other times, the consequences are relational, as they damage our marriage, our friendships, our career. When we fornicate, we sin against our own bodies. That means the unintended consequences come into our bodies. Diseases, unwanted or unplanned pregnancies, broken hearts, or emotional drama are all a part of sinning against our bodies.

As in all things, we must set boundaries to protect ourselves and our marriages. Boundaries are in place to help us, not to harm us. They exist to keep us safe and to protect our intimate relationship with our spouse.

ANCHOR LINE 6

Sex and Romance

While there can be sex without love, there is no real love in a marriage relationship without sex. Intimacy brings about physical, emotional, and spiritual bonding. It is an expression of our love for each other, but just as it was created to bring a husband and wife closer together, it can be used to tear them apart—sometimes well before the marriage has even taken place.

This is why, when we are single, we must establish personal boundaries on sex. Then, once we are married, we must refine those boundaries to include the marriage relationship, for a husband needs to seek to sexually please his wife, and the wife her husband. This is how God intended sex to be (1 Corinthians 7:3–4)!

Let's ignore the lies from the world around us, telling us that true holiness is in celibacy while true sexual freedom is in multiple partners. Let's chase after holiness and freedom within the God-ordained confines of marriage. Only then will we be able to create a strong anchor line of sex and romance, resulting in a lasting and fulfilling marriage relationship.

Workbook

Chapter Six Questions

Question: What are some lies about sex that have been taught by the church? What are some lies taught by the world? What does the Bible teach and what are biblically healthy attitudes toward marital intimacy?

Question: What wrong attitudes about sex have entered into your marriage? (This could be baggage from past relationships, wrong teaching you have believed, attitudes or actions your parents displayed, etc.) How can you work together to restore a healthy biblical view of sex to your own marriage?

Action: Talk together (remember reflective listening!) about your needs and dreams when it comes to sex and romance. What is one practical way you can better meet your spouse's needs in these areas? What is something that is going well in your sex life, and how can you build on that strength?

Action: Look back at the five approaches to romance and choose one to focus on this week. How will you romance your spouse in a tangible way? How can these approaches to romance also carry over into your sex life?

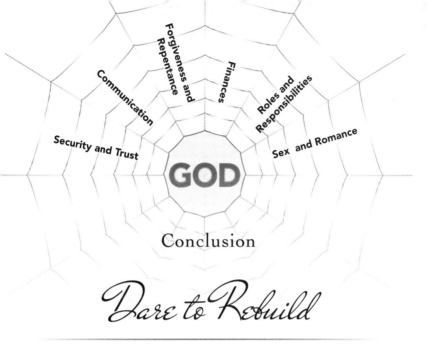

Conclusion

Dare to Rebuild

Do you recall the two spider webs inside my barn? The one was securely anchored and was able to withstand a devastating storm. The other blew away. It didn't have the proper anchor lines to keep it in place. But here's the best part of the story—spiders are extremely adaptable creatures.

Though that spider may have lost her web during the storm, there is a good chance that she made it through and, as soon as the skies cleared and the sun came out, she set about to making another web; this time, stronger and better than the first.

This is your chance to strengthen your web and, if necessary, build an entirely new web altogether within your marriage.

You may feel overwhelmed at the thought of securing these six anchor lines, and if you are planning to do so on your own, then I would agree with you. It's an overwhelming, seemingly impossible task. But God is here to help.

With God at the center of your marriage, you can lean into Him for strength as you work with your spouse to cultivate a healthy relationship. God wants you to have a strong marriage. He wants you to secure these six key anchor lines of security and trust, communication, forgiveness and repentance, finances, roles and responsibilities, and sex and romance.

The marriage relationship is first built on *security and trust* and developing a shared commitment and understanding toward the relationship. You and your spouse must recognize the need to look to God for help and direction with any problem as you work through challenges in life.

Next, you can build a strong marriage through *communication*. Many problems come from miscommunication; therefore, God desires communication to be simple. There are four elements for effective communication we can glean from biblical principles—taking turns talking about each other's needs, listening to each other so that you seek to understand, offering feedback for mutual understanding, and being honest with each other. This anchor line is so important because it is connected to all the other lines. We must communicate effectively to strengthen the other anchor lines.

The third anchor line, *forgiveness and repentance*, is often hard to do. As you communicate more, you will be made aware of issues that need to be repented of and forgiven. This will allow you to prove your dedicated love to each other. Satan will use the act of unforgiveness to put a wedge in your marriage relationship, so by releasing your spouse from their debt and forgiving them or repenting of a wrong, you will reestablish trust in the relationship.

Establishing trust in the relationship is vital when dealing with *finances*. Money is often what drives couples apart, so securing healthy finances in your marriage will take effort from both husband and wife. To prevent serious issues in your marriage, discuss each other's values and develop a budget that seeks to meet both of your needs as well as the needs within the home. Exercising good stewardship will help you learn how to handle your money wisely as a couple.

As a couple, you will also face the reality of *roles and responsibilities*. Establishing these is vital to eliminating stress within the marriage. By understanding each other's roles and how God created both husband and wife with unique needs and strengths, you can better contribute to the relationship.

Within the marriage relationship, God created the need for *sex and romance*, as this is designed to be the ultimate expression of love and commitment between two people. By romancing one another and showing love and respect, you can deepen your intimacy and have a happier, healthier marriage.

These six anchor lines will change your marriage. They will set you up to weather the worst of life's storms. Sure, your web may become damaged here or there, but even if one strand breaks, these anchor lines will ensure that you have plenty more strands to hold things together while you repair the damage and move forward.

As you strengthen your marriage, you will also find that you strengthen your family. Your relationships with loved ones will deepen, and you may notice that your children will respond to you differently. In fact, raising godly children is a seventh anchor line, a topic for another book. But suffice it to say that your marriage relationship has an enormous impact on your children's marriage relationships. Who you are today can influence who they will be thirty years from now.

Our impact on our children is why these anchor lines are so very important. It's not just about finding happiness within our marriages. It's about impacting future generations by modeling what a godly, Christ-filled, healthy marriage looks like.

It all starts with securing that first line. Dare to trust God. Dare to rebuild your web or strengthen each line.

About Duane Sheriff

Duane Sheriff is the founding pastor and senior elder of Victory Life Church, a growing multi-campus church where he served as the senior pastor for over 30 years. His passion is to see people discover their true identity and help them grow in Christ. From the inception of his teaching ministry, this passion has compelled him to make his teachings available free. He enjoys hunting and spending time with his family, especially the grandkids.

The Harrison House Vision

Proclaiming the truth and the power
of the Gospel of Jesus Christ with excellence.

Challenging Christians

to live victoriously,

grow spiritually,

know God intimately.

Harrison
House

Connect with us on

f Facebook @ **HarrisonHousePublishers**

and 📷 Instagram @ **HarrisonHousePublishing**

so you can stay up to date with news

about our books and our authors.

Visit us at **www.harrisonhouse.com**

for a complete product listing as well as

monthly specials for wholesale distribution.

Nico + Sarah Sexual Boundaries

- No being in each other's room w/o someone in there with us
- No doing something we wouldn't do in front of family
-